The Southeast

Lorin Driggs

Consultants

Jennifer L. Brown, Ed.S.
Educational Specialist, Elementary Social Studies
Fairfax County Public Schools, Virginia

T. McCoy-Thomas, Ph.D.
Curriculum Supervisor, Social Studies
East Baton Rouge Parish Public Schools, Louisiana

Tony Disario
Social Studies Coordinator
Griffin Spalding County Schools, Georgia

Brian Allman
Principal
Upshur County Schools, West Virginia

Publishing Credits

Rachelle Cracchiolo, M.S.Ed., *Publisher*
Emily R. Smith, M.A.Ed., *SVP of Content Development*
Véronique Bos, *VP of Creative*
Dona Herweck Rice, *Senior Content Manager*
Dani Neiley, *Editor*
Fabiola Sepulveda, *Series Graphic Designer*

Image Credits: p10-13 paintings by Martin Pate, Newnan GA Courtesy of Southeastern Archaeological Center NPS and Louisiana Office of State Parks; p14 Sarin Images/Granger; p17 Sarin Images/Granger; p19 Cecil Stoughton/White House Press Office; p21 The White House; p23 David R. Frazier/ DanitaDelimont.com/ "Danita Delimont Photography"/Newscom; p32 Shutterstock/Xackery Irving; all other images from iStock and/or Shutterstock

Library of Congress Cataloging-in-Publication Data

Names: Driggs, Lorin, author.
Title: The Southeast / Lorin Driggs.
Description: Huntington Beach, CA : Teacher Created Materials, [2023] | Includes index. | Audience: Grades 4-6 | Summary: "You are invited on a tour of the southeastern United States. Visit mountains, caves, and seashores. Learn about its people and its history. Understand why slavery played such a big role in the Southeast. Discover how the place and its people have changed over time"-- Provided by publisher.
Identifiers: LCCN 2022021241 (print) | LCCN 2022021242 (ebook) | ISBN 9781087690995 (paperback) | ISBN 9781087691152 (ebook)
Subjects: LCSH: Southern States--History--Juvenile literature.
Classification: LCC F209.3 .D75 2023 (print) | LCC F209.3 (ebook) | DDC E467--dc23/eng/20220503
LC record available at https://lccn.loc.gov/2022021241
LC ebook record available at https://lccn.loc.gov/2022021242

Shown on the cover is the Savannah National Wildlife Refuge.

This book may not be reproduced or distributed in any way without prior written consent from the publisher.

5482 Argosy Avenue
Huntington Beach, CA 92649
www.tcmpub.com

ISBN 978-1-0876-9099-5
© 2023 Teacher Created Materials, Inc.

Table of Contents

Welcome to the Southeast 4
The Shape of the Land 6
Indigenous Peoples 10
The Way It Was 14
Civic Life 20
A Changing Economy 22
Home Sweet Home 26
Map It! 28
Glossary 30
Index 31
Learn More! 32

Welcome to the Southeast

Imagine you want to take a summer vacation in the United States. You have a list of things you would like to do and places you would like to see. Exploring and enjoying nature is the first thing on your list. A long hike on a cool mountain trail would be great. Along the way, you would like to stop and have a picnic near a beautiful waterfall. You have always wanted to visit a cave. A chance to see alligators in the wild would be great, too. Next comes enjoying the sun and surf on a warm, sandy beach. That means your trip will include a visit to the coast.

Your trip is not just about outdoor activities and relaxing, though. History is on your list, too. You are interested in the **cultures** of Indigenous peoples. You are curious about early European colonies, too. Finally, you want to learn more about the civil rights movement in the United States.

Is there a part of the country where you can do all of these things without having to travel long distances? Yes! The 12 states of the Southeast included in this book will let you check off everything on your list. They are Alabama, Arkansas, Florida, Georgia, Kentucky, Louisiana, Mississippi, North Carolina, South Carolina, Tennessee, Virginia, and West Virginia.

Southeast Superlatives

The largest house in America is the Biltmore House in North Carolina. The most visited U.S. national park is Great Smoky Mountains National Park in Tennessee and North Carolina. The most visited theme park in the world is Disney's Magic Kingdom in Florida.

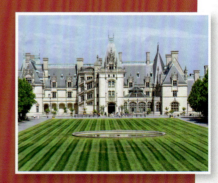

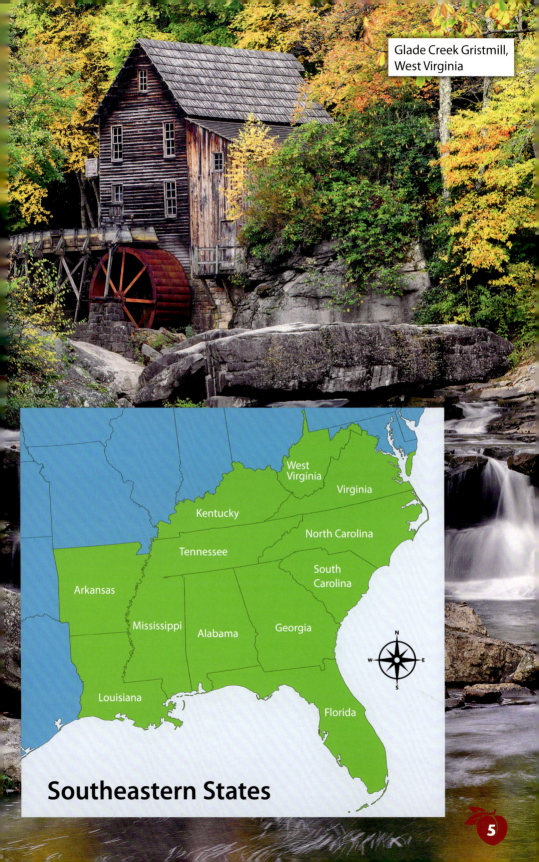
Glade Creek Gristmill, West Virginia

Southeastern States

The Shape of the Land

Geography has always shaped the lives of people. Long ago, it affected almost everything people did. The features of the land determined what people ate, the clothes they wore, and where and how they could travel. Today, geography offers more opportunities than limits.

The geography of the Southeast is as varied as any region in the United States. The land changes from north to south and east to west. Its mountains, valleys, coastlines, lakes, rivers, and wetlands have great natural beauty. It has wonderful places to live, work, and have fun. The climate is relatively mild.

Mountains and Hills

The Appalachian Mountains stretch through nine of the twelve states in the Southeast. They continue northward into Canada. The Great Smoky Mountains and the Blue Ridge Mountains are part of the Appalachian range. Mount Mitchell in North Carolina is the highest peak in the eastern United States. Mountaintops in the Appalachians tend to be rounded or domed rather than jagged. This is a clue to their age. They are among the oldest mountains on Earth.

East and south of the mountains is a region called the Piedmont. The name comes from two Italian words that mean "foot" and "hill." This land has low hills and narrow valleys. The rivers and streams that flow here create many waterfalls.

Mount Mitchell, North Carolina

Appalachian Music

There is a particular kind of music that started in the Appalachian Mountains. It is called *Bluegrass*. Bluegrass music is related to music from England, Ireland, and Scotland. It is usually played with a banjo, a fiddle, and other stringed instruments.

Long Coastline

Eight of the twelve southeastern states touch the Atlantic Ocean or the Gulf of Mexico. The land from the Piedmont to the coast is called the *coastal plain*. It is mostly low and flat. There are swamps and marshes there. Along the coast, there are sandy beaches, bays, and nearby islands.

Rivers and Lakes

The Southeast has many large rivers and lakes. The Mississippi River is known as America's mighty river. It starts in the north, but it passes through or along the borders of 10 states: Minnesota, Wisconsin, Iowa, Illinois, Missouri, Kentucky, Tennessee, Arkansas, Mississippi, and Louisiana. Before it empties into the Gulf of Mexico, the river opens into Lake Pontchartrain in southeastern Louisiana. This is the second-largest lake in the Southeast. The largest lake in the region is Lake Okeechobee in Florida. Water from that shallow lake flows out into the vast wetlands called the Everglades.

Hallandale coastline, Florida

Climate and Weather

A tropical hurricane approaches the Southeast.

The climate of the Southeast is relatively mild. States in the northern part have more seasonal changes than those in the south. They often have snow in the winter, for example. Some states farther south can have warm weather year-round.

The Southeast's long coastline has many advantages. But being near the coast can be a problem, too. The main problem is hurricanes. They affect the Southeast more than any other region of the United States.

Mammoth Cave

Mammoth Cave National Park in Kentucky is home to the longest cave system in the world. More than 400 miles (644 kilometers) of the system have been explored and mapped. Among the animals that live in the cave are bats, shrimp, and eyeless fish.

Indigenous Peoples

People lived in the Southeast thousands of years before the land came to be called America. They had beliefs, governments, and **traditions**. They built cities and knew how to use the natural resources in the land to meet their needs. They knew how to survive.

At least 25 different **native** groups called the Southeast home. The people lived, loved, worked, built, played, and traveled. Their cultures were thousands of years old.

drawing of Poverty Point Mounds

Mysterious Mounds

Mounds built by early native peoples varied in size and shape. Scientists believe the flat-topped mounds were used for buildings, such as temples and homes of chiefs. Dome-shaped mounds were used for burials. The tallest dome is about 72 feet (22 meters) high!

Poverty Point Culture

The native peoples known as the Poverty Point culture lived in what is now Louisiana and Mississippi. The name comes from the place where evidence of this **civilization** was found.

These people got food by fishing, hunting, and gathering plants that grew in the wild. They made tools and other objects from stone. They traded with other native groups.

The Poverty Point peoples built large mounds of earth in their communities. Many mounds still exist. The mounds were probably burial places. They were clearly an important part of their culture. Scientists are still studying them to learn more.

Poverty Point men fishing from their canoes

Adena Culture

This group is named for where evidence of their culture was found. They lived in parts of Kentucky and West Virginia. They hunted, fished, and gathered wild plants for food. They grew some of their food as well, including squash and sunflowers.

The Adena peoples built mounds, too. **Archaeologists** are still trying to understand all the uses of the mounds.

Mississippian Culture

The Mississippian culture was made up of different groups who shared some of the same beliefs and practices. Their communities were in several southeastern states. Most built towns and villages in river valleys where the soil was good. They were farmers. They grew corn, squash, beans, and other crops. They also gathered wild plants. They fished and hunted as well. Like earlier cultures in the region, they built huge earthen mounds that were used for burials and other purposes.

Mississippian village

Mississippian peoples

Native Tribes

In time, the native peoples formed cultural and family groups known as tribes. Among the tribes of the Southeast were the Biloxi, Chickasaw, Choctaw, Creek, Cherokee, Miccosukee, Seminole, and Tunica peoples, as well as others. Each tribe had its own traditions, stories, songs, language, and ways of life.

Members of the tribes lived in villages of a few hundred people. They shared resources and lived **communally**. While they had social structures with leaders, the people mainly worked together to survive and thrive.

River Art

Many of the tribes in the Southeast used river cane as an important material for weaving. River cane is a type of bamboo that grows thickly. It is a naturally strong material. The tribes wove baskets, containers for food storage, and ceremonial items such as rattles.

The Way It Was

The history of the Southeast is one of ancient cultures and new beginnings. It is about danger and discovery. It is about change and growth.

The Southeast has always been important in American history. Four of the first thirteen states are in the Southeast. George Washington and other great leaders came from the region. In fact, four of the first five presidents were from Virginia alone.

Newcomers

The arrival of Europeans brought big changes to the Southeast. Explorers and then colonists came. This "New World" seemed full of opportunities. They wanted to make the land their own.

Explorers from Spain reached what is now Florida in the early 1500s. In 1565, Spain established the first European settlement there. They called it St. Augustine. England established Roanoke Colony in 1585 in what is now North Carolina. Jamestown, Virginia, was established in 1607.

More and more Europeans arrived. Sometimes, the native peoples welcomed them. Other times, they fought. The colonists wanted land. The native peoples needed to protect their ways of life.

Sir Walter Raleigh in Roanoke

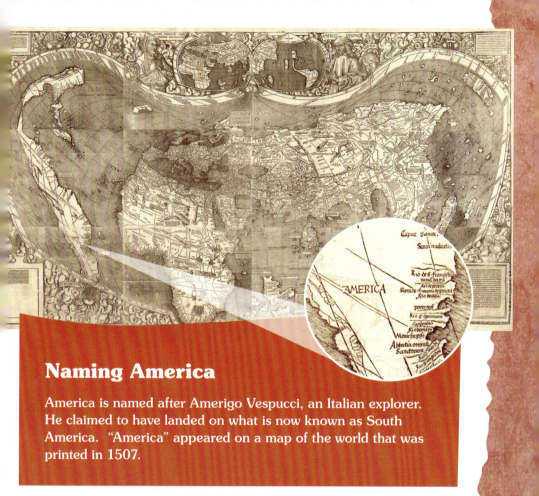

Naming America

America is named after Amerigo Vespucci, an Italian explorer. He claimed to have landed on what is now known as South America. "America" appeared on a map of the world that was printed in 1507.

Fighting for Land

After the American Revolution, the new nation worked to expand its land and resources. In 1830, the U.S. government passed the Indian Removal Act. This law said that the native peoples had to give up their land in the Southeast. In exchange, the government would give them land west of the Mississippi River. When American Indians refused the deal, soldiers forced them to leave. The peoples had to walk to the new "Indian Territory." It was as long as 5,000 miles (8,047 kilometers) away in what is now Oklahoma. The Cherokee called this the "Trail of Tears." It is estimated that between 5,000 and 15,000 people died on the journey.

New Nation, Old Trouble

In 1619, the European colonists also brought slavery to the New World as a business practice. This practice became a major part of life in the Southeast and shaped the region's history in a powerful way. Countless numbers of **enslaved** people were forced to American shores.

Slavery existed in the Southeast from early on. The climate there was ideal for growing cotton and other cash crops. Eventually, the Southeast chose to depend on these crops and the practice of slavery. Enslaved people were forced to do the work. Without them, the **economy** would fail.

The North and the South battle during the Civil War.

From the beginning, people of the new nation were divided in their views on slavery. By 1804, all Northern states had voted to abolish the institution of slavery. In 1860, Abraham Lincoln was elected president. Many people thought he was against slavery. That put pressure on government leaders across the South. They responded in a big way. Eleven states decided to secede, or leave the United States in 1861.

Lincoln believed the split would destroy American **democracy**. He said the nation was "the last best hope." He could not allow it to fail.

The North and South went to war. This Civil War lasted four years. During the war, President Lincoln signed the Emancipation Proclamation, an order freeing all enslaved people in non-Union states. Two years later, the South surrendered. As a result of the war, slavery was ended.

Juneteenth

It took two years for news to reach the enslaved people of Texas that they had been freed. Union soldiers delivered the news on June 19, 1865. June 19 came to be called Juneteenth. Now, that is the name of the holiday that celebrates the freedom of the enslaved people.

Change and Growth

After the war, Southern states had to do certain things as they rejoined the United States. Each state had to write a new **constitution**. A majority of voters had to approve it, including African Americans. They also had to accept the terms of three **amendments** to the U.S. Constitution. One abolished slavery. The second granted citizenship to formerly enslaved people. The third guaranteed the right to vote for formerly enslaved men. By 1870, all the states had met the requirements. But the discrimination and segregation continued throughout the South.

Louisiana's Constitution

Fastest Growing

By the early 2020s, the Southeast had become the fastest growing region in the country. It has grown in population and political power.

Atlanta, Georgia

President Lyndon Johnson signs the Civil Rights Act as Dr. Martin Luther King Jr. and others look on.

Civil Rights

By the mid-1900s, a growing number of people started a new movement that centered in the Southeast. The civil rights movement worked to end the legacy of slavery. African Americans demanded equal rights. The movement made progress, but it was slow.

African Americans fought for their rights in court and won. Black **activists** and their supporters boycotted places and services that discriminated. They held non-violent protests. They voted. These are the rights of citizens.

More victories followed. One was the Civil Rights Act of 1964. It banned discrimination based on race. People of all races in the South today enjoy the rights of citizens. They vote and are elected to government offices. People of all backgrounds live and work together as equals.

Civic Life

Throughout the Southeast, civic life is much like it is throughout the rest of the United States. People vote, protest, demonstrate for causes, and run for office. The people elect their leaders and have a say in laws and practices in their areas.

Historically, the Southeast was heavily imbalanced as to who had a say and who did not. That has changed over time. New **federal** laws created some of these changes in the Southeast. But also, the people of the Southeast have worked for equality and **representation** for all. Organizations supporting equality are strong in the Southeast. Community organizers and others work to encourage people in all communities to vote and be involved. More and more diverse people have been elected to important offices. Many people work together to get everyone's voices heard.

Children participate in "My Voice Matters" at the 50th anniversary of the March on Washington.

The Southeast has also produced some of the country's most important leaders. Eight U.S. presidents were born in Virginia, and six of those were among the first ten presidents. Fourteen presidents in all have been from the Southeast, including the great leader and Kentucky native, Abraham Lincoln.

President Barack Obama honors Senator John Lewis with the Presidential Medal of Freedom.

Activist, Leader, Legislator

John Lewis served 17 terms representing Georgia in the U.S. Congress. Before he became a politician, he was a civil rights activist who worked alongside Martin Luther King Jr. He was the youngest speaker at the 1963 March on Washington.

A Changing Economy

The economy of the Southeast is as varied as its geography. In fact, the land plays a big role in many parts of the economy.

Products from the Earth

The southern states' long summers and mild winters are great for growing crops. There is usually plenty of rain. It helps that much of the land is flat. The soil is generally **fertile**. Cotton, tobacco, and rice were the main crops in earlier times. They are still important, but there are other key crops now. These include hay, wheat, and sugarcane. Vegetables and legumes are also important crops, including corn, peanuts, and soybeans. When it comes to fruit, you may have heard that Georgia is known for its peaches. But peanuts, pecans, and blueberries are the most produced crops in the state. Peaches are Georgia's state fruit, so they are still important. Florida is known for oranges and other citrus fruits.

Georgia peach trees

Raising chickens for meat and eggs is big business in the Southeast. Cattle and pigs are also raised. The meatpacking **industry** is a significant source of jobs.

West Virginia and Kentucky are two major producers of coal. **Minerals** used in making modern electronics are also mined in the region. Phosphate is a mineral used to make fertilizer for plants. It is mined in Florida and North Carolina.

chicken farm

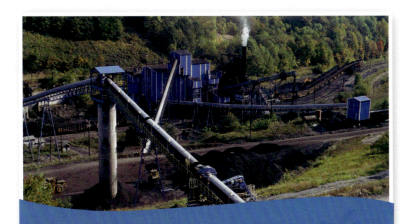

Future of Coal

Burning coal to generate energy is a source of pollution and contributes to climate change. The lack of demand has caused coal mining in the Southeast and elsewhere to drop sharply. Thousands of coal miners are unemployed.

Industries Move South

After the Civil War, agriculture was still big in the Southeast. But there were now many more workers who needed jobs. Business owners saw an opportunity for cheap labor. And there was a lot of space to build factories. By the 1920s, the South became a center for producing yarn, cloth, and clothing. More jobs came later with the car industry. Today, there are factories throughout the region. Big cities attract banking and other businesses that employ office workers.

The entertainment industry has come to the Southeast. The region has good locations for filming movies and TV shows. The costs are also much lower than in New York and California.

A film crew works on a movie set in the Southeast.

People Go South

The Southeast's population is growing. More and more people go there for jobs. The cost of living is lower than in some other areas. The nice weather helps, too. These new residents need places to live, work, and shop. That is good for real estate and construction.

Tourism is huge in the economy of the Southeast. Every state has at least one large theme park. There are also many national parks in the region. Hiking, camping, swimming, boating, fishing, golfing, and relaxing in nature are available all year.

Universal Studios in Orlando, Florida

Sun Belt, Here We Come

Most of the Southeast states, except Virginia, West Virginia, and Kentucky, are in the country's Sun Belt. It is called this because of the year-round mild weather there. Southern sunshine has always tempted people to abandon the North's cold winters. In the past, people who moved there were mainly retirees. Now, people of all ages are heading to the lower Southeast.

a beach in Alabama

Home Sweet Home

Native peoples first made the Southeast their home thousands of years ago. They knew how to live on the land. They created a successful way of life. Europeans arrived about 500 years ago. They had different skills and beliefs. They, too, created a successful way of life.

Conflict between old and new is a theme of the region's history. Indigenous peoples and European colonists fought over land and culture for many years. Unfortunately, over time, many native tribes and nations lost their homelands and migrated west.

The cruel practice of slavery also caused conflict. It nearly broke the nation. Americans went to war with other Americans. Legal slavery ended, but discrimination against African Americans did not. The struggle for equality isn't fully over, and people are continuing to fight.

Frankfort, Kentucky

That Southern Accent

Southern accents may all sound the same to people from outside the Southeast. In fact, they vary greatly in different parts of the Southeast, which is a huge area. Experts believe their basic characteristics are closer to a British accent than any other American accent.

Business in the region is growing. The climate and economic opportunities attract more and more new residents. However, some groups of people have benefited less than others from the new opportunities. This is a challenge that many regional leaders are addressing.

Old ways and new ideas can coexist. The Southeast holds on to many cultural gifts from the past. At the same time, it embraces a new, modern identity. The people who live and work there are ready for a diverse and positive future.

Map It!

The Southeast has something for everyone when it comes to fun. Work with a group to create a Southeast map that shows where people can enjoy particular activities.

1. Make a map of the Southeast that shows all 12 states. Label the capitals and a few big cities in each state.
2. Review this book, and do some research online and in other books. Look for activities that are popular in each of the states.
3. Make a list of the types of activities and places you want to add to your map. Here are some examples: climbing a mountain, touring a cave, visiting a theme park, swimming in a lake, seeing an alligator, catching a fish, and going to a beach. Be sure to add your own ideas.
4. Talk with each other about ways you could show the places and activities. For example, you could draw little pictures. You could label them with words. You could use different colors for different kinds of activities.
5. Work together to make your map.
6. When the map is finished, share it with your whole class.

The Blowing Rock, North Carolina

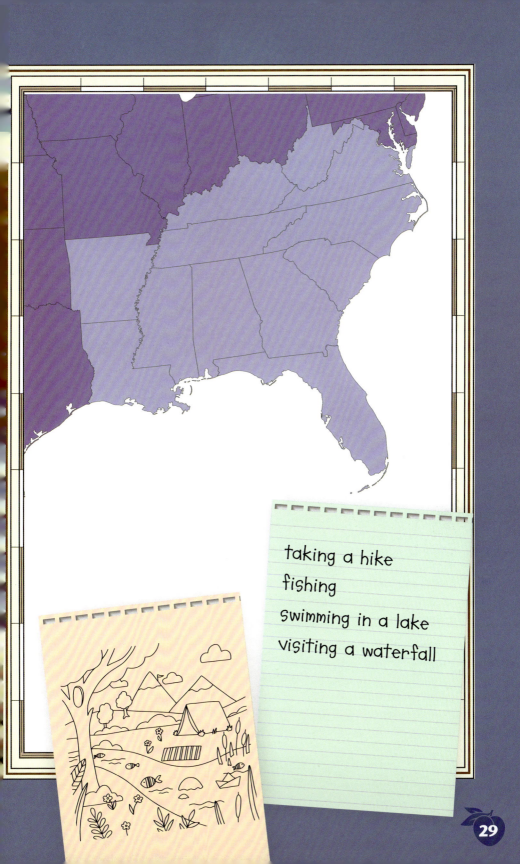

Glossary

activists—people who take strong action to make changes in politics or society

amendments—changes in the words of a law or document

archaeologists—scientists who learn about past human life by studying objects that ancient people left behind

civilization—an organized society with particular beliefs and ways of living

communally—actively sharing and interacting together

constitution—a document that describes the laws and the system of government for a country, state, or organization

cultures—the beliefs, customs, and forms of art of societies, groups, places, or time periods

democracy—a form of government in which people choose leaders by voting

economy—the system of making, selling, and buying goods and services in a particular place

enslaved—owned by another person and forced to work without pay

federal—relating to the United States or other national government

fertile—able to produce many plants or crops

industry—a group of businesses that provide a particular product or service

minerals—substances that occur naturally, usually in the ground

native—born or existing naturally in a particular place

representation—the act of speaking or acting for a person or group of people so they can be represented in a legislative body

tourism—the activity of traveling to a place for pleasure

traditions—customs and beliefs that are passed down in families or other groups of people

Index

Adena culture, 12

American Indians, 14–15, 26

Appalachian Mountains, 6–7

Atlantic Ocean, 8

Biltmore House, 4

Blue Ridge Mountains, 6

Cherokee, 13, 15

Civil Rights Act of 1964, 19

Civil War, 17, 24

Everglades, 8

Great Smoky Mountains, 4, 6

Gulf of Mexico, 8

Indian Removal Act, 15

Indian Territory, 15

Jamestown, 14

Juneteenth, 17

Lake Okeechobee, 8

Lake Pontchartrain, 8

Lewis, John, 21

Lincoln, Abraham, 17, 21

Magic Kingdom, 4

Mammoth Cave, 9

Mississippian culture, 12–13

Mississippi River, 8, 15

New World, 14, 16

Oklahoma, 15

Piedmont, 6, 8

Poverty Point culture, 11

Spain, 14

St. Augustine, 14

Sun Belt, 25

Vespucci, Amerigo, 15

Washington, George, 14

Learn More!

John Lewis had many roles in the civil rights movement. Conduct research to learn about his life, from his birth to his death.

- Create a time line of the significant moments in his life.

- Include quotations from Lewis.

- Also include interesting facts about his life and accomplishments. Be sure to explain what he meant by "good trouble."